Capital Wise

DON'T CALL IT A BUDGET

Personal Money Planning in the age of STUFF Overload

Introduction

Welcome to the wonderful world of personal budgeting!

Before you think we're crazy, let us ask you:

- Are you feeling in despair – or worse, panicking – about your personal finances?
- Do you feel that your spending is out of control, but you don't know what to do about it?
- Are you having a hard time keeping up with your credit card payments?
- Do you find that you are just breaking even, and can't save to meet your financial goals?

Notice those words: despair, panic, out of control, hard time, can't save. Nothing there about peace of mind! Your spending problems are understandable. Most people in the 21st century, no matter what their income, want products and services that did not necessarily exist in generations past, when savings levels were higher. Things like technology in all of its forms, coffee on the go, personally financed retirements, even air conditioning, are all considered essential now, and must be paid for. And yet, our incomes don't always keep pace with the cost of these new "necessities" of life.

You have come to the right place. We have developed this workbook to provide you with a step-by-step process to:

1) discover where your money has been going,
2) figure out where and how you can make better spending choices, and
3) put a framework in place to repair your financial picture, then make it beautiful.

This framework can be called a budget. But "budget" is kind of a downer word, as it connotes lack of freedom, and denial of fun things. This is unfortunate, because the budgets we have in mind do the opposite. That's because, when you have strategies in place to control your spending (that is, choose - not deny!), boost your savings for future goals, and, in general, have your money working for you, you will realize that, far from being a drudgery, a good budget will give you confidence, relief, control, and peace of mind.

So, let's drop the "B" word, and instead of "Budget", let's call it your Personal Money Plan, or PMP.

And let's get started now.

Table of Contents

SECTION I

A SNAPSHOT OF YOUR FINANCES

1. <u>What Are You Worth Today?</u>

Before we start working on your Personal Money Plan (PMP), we first want to ask you, what are you worth financially; that is, how much wealth do you have? Why start there? Because your ultimate goal is to increase your financial worth, or wealth, right? Your PMP will be a tool to help you increase your financial worth. How do you know if your financial worth is increasing? You measure it from time to time, say, every year on December 31, or on your birthday. How do you measure it? That's what we will do in this section. We will show you how to measure your financial worth.

Let's begin with some definitions. Financial worth is different than how much money you have. It also takes into account what you owe. When we measure someone's financial worth, we note everything they own that has financial value (these are called Assets), on one side of the page, and everything they owe (called Liabilities or Debt), on the other side. The difference between what you own and what you owe is called your "net worth", which is the same as your financial worth, or wealth. (In business, they call the document that lists what a company owns, what it owes, and what the difference is, a "balance sheet".) Note that you measure financial worth at a point in time. So, each time you do it is like a snapshot. You retain these snapshots and compare them over time, to see if your wealth is growing.

So, let's start with the "what you own", or Asset, side of the chart on page 13. You should include everything of reasonable value here. Usually, you would start by listing your financial assets – money in bank accounts, for example. We hope you aren't hiding money in your mattress, but, if you are, include that too. You can use our form below, which has many common asset categories, or you can rename categories that reflect your own assets. Just make sure the column on the left includes all of your things that have value.

Now, pause a moment. Financial asset values are pretty easy to figure out. Your bank's or brokerage firm's website will tell you what your account values are on a given date. But what about your non-financial assets? The china that your Aunt Clara gave you certainly has value. And you should include it. However, you need to make a reasonable assumption about what you might get for it if you sold it on eBay or Craigslist, because that is the true measure of what it is worth financially today. You don't want to drive yourself crazy doing this, so you should really only include non-financial assets that could readily be converted into cash. Include the trade-in value of your car. Include very valuable jewelry (but only at the eBay value!) and high-value antique furniture (ditto) and your comic book collection, but only if it has substantial current sale value. If you own a home, include it at what you think is its current market value.

Okay, now that your assets are all organized, let's move to the right side of the page, and list what you owe. All of those credit card balances get listed here. As does your mortgage, if you have one. Car loans get listed here. And student loans. And money you owe to family members or friends.

If you have a home equity line of credit (HELOC) and have used it, whatever amount you owe should be included. Any amount you owe anyone or any company or any institution gets listed.

Now, the math equation. Look at your total Assets at the bottom of the left column and subtract your total Debt from the right column and write down the number next to where it says "Net Worth". Congratulations, you have done your first financial worth statement. Don't lose it. You will be comparing future statements with it.

"Excuse me", you say, "but my number is negative". Yes, it happens. It will happen to many people who are starting out on their PMP journey. What this means is that what you owe to others is larger than the value of everything you own. How do you make that number positive, and keep it increasing over time? You put together a strong Personal Money Plan and you live by it.

So, let's do it.

Personal Balance Sheet

What you own:		What you owe:	
"Cash" Assets		Current Debt	
Checking		Credit Card Balances	
Savings		Loans from Friends & Family	
Total "Cash" Assets		Total Current Debt	
Home-related Assets		Long-Term Debt	
Home/other Real Estate		Mortgages	
Car		Home Equity Loan	
Furniture/other		Car Loans	
Total Home-related Assets		Student Loans	
		Personal Loans	
Investment Assets		Total Long Term Debt	
Stocks/Bonds			
Mutual Funds		Other Debt	
Retirement: IRA/401(k)/403(b)			
Total Investment Assets		**TOTAL DEBT**	
Other: cash value life insurance/loans			
to others/cash value pension/ other assets		**NET WORTH (Total Assets minus Total Debt)**	
TOTAL ASSETS			

2. How Much Do You Earn?

Essential to a strong Personal Money Plan is understanding your "cash flow" - that is, how much you earn and how much you spend. Once you know those things, your Plan becomes how you increase your earnings and manage your spending. You are then in control of the plan – by increasing earnings and/or reducing spending, you increase your net worth, or wealth, that we discussed in the previous section. Then you have the happy task of deciding how to use that wealth to reach your financial goals.

But, we are getting ahead of ourselves. Let's start with earnings. What do you earn? More specifically, what is your spendable income, that is, what do you earn that is available to be spent or saved? Our monthly income worksheet on page 17 will help you figure that out. Start with what you get paid from your primary job, whether it's a salary, or self-employment income, or whatever. Subtract out the deductions that come out of each paycheck before you even see it – Federal taxes, state and local taxes, employment taxes, Medicare taxes, and other deductions. Perhaps your company has a savings plan or 401(k) plan that you contribute to from each paycheck. You should subtract those amounts as well.

"Wait a minute", you say. "Why am I deducting savings and 401(k) payments, when that's my money?" Good question. It's because you have already accounted for them in your financial worth statement in the previous section. Those paycheck deductions are part of your financial assets, and they are safely noted on your financial worth statement. Therefore, we can't count them again now, since they are not going to be part of your spendable income, or "cash flow". List all your other sources of income on the worksheet, like income from a second job, alimony, interest, dividends, bonus payments (lucky you !), pension income, Social Security income, and so on. But remember, you must subtract taxes you will owe from all of these income sources, even if they don't deduct taxes for you. We have listed the typical deductions that will be taken from your salary. You should take appropriate deductions from your other income sources as well. For example, income taxes (federal, state, possibly local) apply to virtually all income sources, and FICA and Medicare taxes may apply too. If you receive Social Security income, you can check irs.gov for information regarding your taxable amount.

One other important note: you are trying to quantify all of your income in a typical month. But much or all of your income may not come to you on a monthly basis. You may get your paycheck bi-weekly and your bonus just once per year. Maybe your interest earnings are paid to you quarterly. To find your monthly amount, first calculate your full year amount, then divide that by 12 to approximate a monthly amount. For example, for your bi-weekly paycheck, multiply each item (salary, federal taxes, state taxes, and so on) by 26 (since you will get 26 bi-weekly paychecks in a full year), then divide each amount by 12 to get a monthly amount to include on the worksheet. (We have not included a bi-weekly column in the chart on page 17, but you can do the calculation and include the monthly equivalents in the Monthly Earnings column). An annual payment, like a bonus, should be divided by 12 to get a monthly amount. A quarterly payment can be multiplied by 4 to find the full year number, then divided by 12 for a monthly. (Or just divide by 3, since a quarterly payment covers 3 months).

Once you have noted all of your income sources and deductions, add columns I, II, and III and record the totals in column IV. The "Total" in the bottom right corner of the chart should be your total monthly spendable income.

Now that you've figured out your income, we'll take a long look at your expenses. But, before we leave income, note that we will come back to this later. If you want to increase your wealth, one way is to increase your income. You may want to think about ways you could do that. Some ways include negotiating for a raise or promotion at work, or moonlighting with a second job (preferably something you love doing, so it won't seem like you're working all the time!). Somebody we know loves to shop at garage sales. She makes money by selling some of her finds on eBay. You may want to start thinking about your own skills and interests, and how you might "monetize" them, or earn something while you enjoy your outside pursuits.

Okay, then. On to spending.

Calculating Your Monthly Cash Flow
First, How Much Do You Earn?

Source	I. Monthly Earnings	II. Quarterly Earnings (divide by 3)	III. Annual Earnings (divide by 12)	IV. Total Earnings (add I, II, III)
A. Gross Salary				
B. Less: All Taxes				
C. After Tax Salary (=A-B)				
D. Less: Benefits (ie. Health, FlexPlans)				
E. Less: Savings (ie. Employer Sponsored Retirement Plans/ Savings Plans)				
F. Less Other				
G. EARNED (Take Home) INCOME (=C-D-E-F)				
OTHER INCOME:				
Add in following *less taxes owed*				
H. Dividends/Interest				
I. Pension				
J. Alimony				
K. Other				
TOTAL SPENDABLE INCOME (=G+H+I+J+K)				

3. How Much Do You Spend?

Spending can be an insidious thing. We know when we spend large amounts from time to time. It's the small, frequent amounts that, when you multiply them by the number of days in a month you spend them, often provoke a "Wow" response. Fancy coffee at $5 per day, 20 working days per month, is $100 per month. Just for coffee.

So, really, the only way to make sure you are accounting for all of your spending, is to keep a daily journal for long enough to cover most everything you purchase. We suggest one month. In our Appendix 5 you will find a Weekly Expense Tracker to get you started. (You may want to make several copies so you can track your spending for several weeks). List everything you pay for every day, whether you use cash, checks or credit cards. Include all of the bills you pay as well. However, credit card bills are a little tricky, since you don't want to double count. Using the coffee example again, if you list that $5 mocha latte every day which you charge to your credit card, and then also include the payment of your credit card bill which probably includes the coffee charges for the prior month, you will be double counting. So, if you pay your credit card balances off in full every month (good for you!), you don't need to note when you pay your credit card bill, because you will be noting all of the individual charges each day.

However, if you do not pay your credit card bill in full each month, but make either minimum payments or a set payment amount each month, you should note that payment. This is because, once you start making partial credit card payments, huge interest rates kick in, and it may take years to pay off your credit card bills at the rate you are paying. So, in effect, your monthly credit card payment becomes just another bill you have to pay. So, do include it. (In a later section, we will strongly encourage you to pay off those credit card bills to stop the killer interest charges, but more on that later....)

In addition to tracking all of your spending for 30 days, you also need to consider spending that happens less frequently, that you may not capture in the 30 days of tracking. For example, consider bills that you receive on a quarterly, semi-annual or annual basis. For these bills, just figure out what the monthly cost would be and include it on one of the days in your tracker. To do that, divide a quarterly bill by 3 to get a monthly amount; divide a semi-annual bill by 6 and divide an annual bill by 12 to get the monthly equivalent amounts. The chart on page 20 can help you record those items.

Then, put the various charges into categories that are meaningful to you. For example, you may want to have a "Food" category that includes groceries, all those coffee drinks, restaurant dining, and so on. If you eat out a lot, you may want a "Grocery" category and a "Restaurant Meals" category (which could include the coffee). A "Car-Related" category would include car maintenance, gasoline, car insurance, and so on. Once you've put all of your expenses into a manageable number of meaningful categories, then just transfer the amounts by category to the chart on page 21. We have provided several common categories of spending for your convenience. However, you should use categories that make sense for your own situation, so feel free to modify our categories as needed. Be sure to hold on to all of the details in your weekly trackers. Later you will be looking for creative ways to reduce spending, that is, to spend less without a lot of pain. You will likely need the tracker details at that point.

You will note in the chart on page 21 that we have used the terms "fixed" and "variable" for our spending categories. We think it's helpful to think about your spending as either "fixed", meaning you are unlikely to be able to reduce that spending in the short to intermediate time frame, or "variable", meaning that you have more control over whether or not you spend in those categories. As examples, rent, especially if you have a signed lease, is "fixed" in the near-term, while entertainment is "variable", since you can choose to do it or not do it at any time.

One final note on spending. In the chart on page 21, we have a category labeled "Fixed: health, life, medical, dental insurance". Since you have already subtracted benefits costs from your income on page 17, do not include those costs again here. However, do include additional related costs, like copays, deductibles, self-paid health expenses, and life insurance premiums.

Now, let's move on to a crucial calculation. What is your "net cash flow", that is, how much is left when you subtract your typical monthly spending from your monthly spendable income?

Quarterly/Annual Bills To Be Added Into Monthly Expenses

Bill	Quarterly/Annual Amount	Monthly Equivalent
Example 1: Life Insurance Premium		
Example 2: Annual Dues		
Example 3: Quarterly Tax payments		
Example 4: Water and Sewer Tax		

Calculating Your Monthly Cash Flow
Second, How Much Do You Spend?

Expenses By Category	Typical Month's Expenses
Fixed: Housing - Rent/mortgage/property taxes	
Fixed: Utilities-telephone/cell/heat/electric /sewer/water/cable TV/ Internet	
Fixed: Transportation (car payment/Insurance)	
Fixed: health, life, medical, dental insurance	
Fixed: dependent care	
Variable: Transportation (gas, oil, repair, parking tolls, transit)	
Variable: Food, Household, Toiletries	
Variable: Education	
Variable: Clothing and Accessories	
Variable: Home Upgrades/Furniture	
Variable: Entertainment/Dining Out	
Variable: Stationery, Gifts, Office	
TOTAL EXPENSES	

4. What Is Your "Bottom Line"?

Now it's time to do a very important calculation. In a typical month, how much does your spendable income exceed your expenses? This difference - called "net cash flow" or your "bottom line" - is the amount that would be available each month for savings, investments or to achieve your specific financial goals.

On the chart on the next page, write in the amount of your total spendable income (that you calculated two sections ago, in the section "How Much Do You Earn?") in the first open space. This is also your total monthly "cash inflow". For cash outflows, add your fixed expenses from the chart on page 21, and note the total where indicated in the chart below. Do the same for your variable expenses from the chart on page 21. Your total cash outflows are the sum of your fixed and variable expenses.

Calculate your "net cash flow", also known as your "bottom line" by subtracting your monthly cash outflows from your monthly cash inflows.

Now, what do you think about that number? It's hard to have an opinion without a financial plan, and we haven't yet worked on your financial plan. But likely, the following are true:

- If your number is positive, good for you. You are living within your income level. However, is it as positive as it could be without causing you to deprive yourself unduly? Is it positive enough to enable you to reach your financial goals within a reasonable period? We will tackle these questions in a later section.
- If your number is negative, uh-oh. This means that each month you are spending more than you are earning. This is not sustainable over the long term. So, how to rein in the spending, again without causing you undue hardship?

We will be giving you some strategies to think about to take charge of your spending. But first, let's talk about credit card debt, and why, though it's very easy to fall into, it's also very difficult to get out of. Paying off credit card debt, unless you pay your bills in full every month, will likely be a significant expense item for you.

Your Monthly Cash Flow Statement
Third, Putting It All Together

Cash Inflows:	Amount
Total Spendable Income (from page 17)	
A. Total Cash Inflows:	
Cash Outflows:	
Fixed Expenses (from page 21)	
Variable Expenses (from page 21)	
B. Total Cash Outflows:	
Net Cash Flow: (A minus B)	

5. What Is Your Credit Card Debt Doing To You?

In the chart on page 25, list each of your credit cards, what your outstanding balance is for each one as of today's date, the interest rate(s) you are currently paying, the minimum payment, and the number of months until you are debt free. Credit card statements should give you all of this information.

In addition to your account summary, account activity, and changes to your account interest rates and terms, your credit card company should provide you with minimum payment information that includes a warning about how long it would take to pay off your credit card if you only make the minimum payment. If you want to calculate this on your own, you can go to an online financial calculator such as finance.yahoo.com/calculator and find the section that asks, "How long will it take to pay off my credit card?". Another source is http://www.bankrate.com/calculators/credit-cards/credit-card- payoff-calculator.aspx. Insert the details from your credit card statement and look at the results.

Let's say you have an outstanding credit card balance of $900, your annual percentage rate is 18%, and your minimum payment percentage is 5%, which totals about $45 per month. If you plug those numbers into the financial calculator, it would take you 2 years to pay that credit card bill and in those two years you would have racked up another $178 in interest charges! Your total cost for whatever you purchased for $900 would end up costing you $1078.

Do you see how much it will cost you and how long it will take you to pay off that debt if you just make the minimum payments? And that assumes you don't make any more purchases !! The problem with credit card debt is that the companies issuing the cards make the most money if you only make the minimum payments. That way they charge you interest on all of your past balances. It's a downward spiral for most people.

Here are some suggestions if you've got a fair amount of credit card debt:

- Go on a credit card "diet". Put those cards away somewhere for however many months it takes you to pay back what you owe in full.
- Pay far more than the minimum payment each month. Ideally, don't charge more than you can pay in full each month. That way, you get the convenience of using the card (and perhaps mileage points, or other incentives) but the credit card company can't charge you any interest. If you can't pay in full, try to pay as much as you can, then pay in full the following month.
- If you have large outstanding balances, chances are you have a lot of "stuff". Consider selling some of your things online, or having a garage sale of things you no longer use. Then take all of the proceeds and use them to pay down your credit card debt in full or in part.

The idea is that you want to get rid of all past credit card debt as fast as you can, then only charge going forward what you can pay in full each month. This may require you to stop all non-critical spending for several months, until all of those balances are paid off. Consider that a financial "diet", before you start moving forward on your Personal Money Plan. You really can't move forward on achieving your financial goals with the noose of credit card debt around your neck.

Drilling Down Your Credit Card Debt as of _____

Name of Credit Card	Balance	Rate	Minimum Payment	Months till debt free
1.				
2.				
3.				
4.				
5.				
6.				
Total Debt		------		

6. What Is Your Other Debt Doing To You?

You may have other debt – like student loans or a mortgage – and you can do the same exercise in the chart below with this debt that you did with the credit card debt. Generally, though, the interest rates on other debt are lower than that on credit cards.

The idea is the same, though. You would like to pay off higher interest rate debt as fast as you can, which means paying more than the minimums each month. However, student loan and mortgage debt may be more manageable for you over time, in that you are not adding to these loans (unless you are still in school) as you do with credit card debt every month that you don't pay your balance in full.

So, you can possibly work on other financial goals while paying off student loans and mortgage loans at the same time. On the other hand, it's difficult to work on other financial goals if you have substantial credit card debt, because of the heavy interest charges. That's why we so strongly urge you to pay off those credit cards as fast as possible.

Drilling Down Other Debt as of _____

Other Debt	Balance	Rate	Payment	Months till debt free
1.				
2.				
3.				
4.				
5.				
6.				
Total Debt				

7. Calculating Your Cash Cushion

There's one other critical step you need to take before we move on to your Personal Money Plan. In addition to paying off your credit card debt, you should make sure you have adequate emergency cash on hand to cover up to 6 months of expenses, in the event you were to lose your income suddenly. Our chart on page 29 will help you figure out the emergency resources you have available. Some of these resources – like retirement plans and certificates of deposit (CD's) – may have penalties associated with tapping them before they mature. So, you don't want to access these resources unless you have a true emergency. However, you should calculate what would theoretically be available – penalties or no penalties – should you have a sudden loss of income.

Your cash assets include any amounts that could be used to cover expenses in an emergency, not including any penalties. So, money in checking and savings accounts should be included. If you have a brokerage account, include what could easily be turned into cash from that account. Include Certificates of Deposit less any applicable penalties. Include retirement accounts that allow premature distributions, less any applicable penalties. If you have insurance policies that have cash values, include the cash values.

Once you've listed all of your cash assets, add them up to find "Total Cash Assets". Go back to your monthly expense calculation and note your "Total Monthly Expenses" on the next line in the chart below. Then multiply your total monthly expenses by 6, which would be the amount you would need to cover 6 months worth of expenses. Compare that amount to your Total Cash Assets number. If Total Cash Assets are equal to or greater than 6 months worth of expenses, good job! If not, then you need to focus on increasing your cash assets until you have at least 6 months worth of expenses covered for emergencies.

We'll give you some ideas on how to do that in the next section.

Cash Cushion as of _____

Source of Cash	Amount
Checking Account	
Savings Account	
Brokerage Accounts (liquid)	
401K	
IRA	
Other	
Other	
A. Total Cash Assets (add all above)	
B. Total Monthly Expenses (from prior worksheet)	
C. Total Monthly Expenses times 6 (months)	
Total Cash Assets less 6 Months of Expenses (A minus C)	

SECTION II

DEVELOPING YOUR PERSONAL MONEY PLAN

1. Identifying Financial Goals

What are your financial goals?

Ok, we hear you, "Where to start?" Well, chances are that your financial goals are wandering around in your head, perhaps over-shadowed by all of the stuff you need to do just to make it through the day. Try to find yourself some quiet time and think about the following: you are reading this because you need some help with your personal finances. If you just keep doing what you are doing, where will you be in a year? 5 years? 10 years? Since you are smart, you understand that doing what you are doing will likely just make the problem worse. To fix the problem you need a plan. And the first step in the plan is to determine what your goals are. That is, what do you want to have happen? "Well", you might say, "don't we all want the same things to happen? I want to have my financial problems disappear, then get rich, then live happily ever after." Ok. Got it. We weren't asking you the right question. A better question is: what are your financial goals that 1) are specific and reasonably attainable given your current and likely future income levels and 2) are sufficiently enticing to you to encourage you to "make them happen"? Only if your goals are specific, attainable and enticing will you want to stick with a plan that makes them happen.

To get you started, we've provided several examples of financial goals in the chart on page 33. It is helpful to think of financial goals in a timeframe: short-term (less than 1 year), intermediate-term (1 to 5 years) and long-term (over 5 years). You can work on all of your goals at the same time; however, the short-term goals you want finished first.

You can have a fairly ambitious list of goals. But not so ambitious that they are unattainable, which will put a real damper on your PMP. And your goals can change. You may want to reevaluate them every year, or more often if life events happen. Your goals should be as specific as you wish to make them enticing (a beach cottage at the Shore; a lime-green convertible; a worry-free retirement). Write them down. This is the first step to achieving them. The second step is to start to dream about them. The third step is to take the required steps to make them happen.

Examples Of Financial Goals

General Financial Goal	Short Term, Medium Term or Long Term
Pay Off Credit Cards	
Set Up Emergency Fund	
Pay Off Student Loans	
Save for College or Kids' College	
Buy a Car/Furniture/Appliances	
Save for Vacation	
Buy a House/2nd House	
Save for Retirement	

2. Dollar Cost Of Your Financial Goals

Financial goals have a dollar cost. Whether you want to buy that special car, or pay off your credit card bills, the cost of that goal is pretty clear. Note each of your goals in the chart below, and the associated cost for each one. (If one of your goals is a worry-free retirement, there are many websites that can help you determine how much you will need to save to achieve that.) Then add the cost to achieve your short-term, intermediate-term, and long-term goals. Divide by the appropriate number of months (you decide the appropriate number - we have just provided assumptions in the chart below). If your monthly goal costs seem overwhelming, take another look at those goals. Are you being unrealistic in your assumptions of what you can achieve? If so, modify your goals until you feel they are attainable. You can always adjust them if you get a big raise, or win the lottery. Meanwhile, you will feel much better working to achieve goals that are realistic. Add up the monthly amounts to meet your short-, medium- and long-term goals, and note the total on the last line.

Financial Goals – Dollar Cost

Short-Term: (less than one year)
1.
2.
3.

     Total Dollar Amount:_____ Divide by 12 for monthly amount: _____

Medium-Term: (one to five years)
1.
2.
3.

     Total Dollar Amount:_____

     Divide by 36 for monthly amount (assuming 3 years):_____

Long-Term: (more than five years)
1.
2.
3.

     Total Dollar Amount:

     Divide by 120 for monthly amount (assuming 10 years):_____

Total Monthly Cost to Meet Goals (add from above): _____

3. Developing a PMP To Meet Your Goals

Now the real fun begins. We need to (actually, you need to) go back to the work you did on your income and expenses. In this section, you want to create a magical document – your Personal Money Plan. When you are done, ideally your income will more than cover your expenses, so much more that you can allocate dollars every month toward your short-, intermediate- and long-term goals, and allocate enough toward those goals such that you achieve your short-term goals within a year or so, your intermediate- term goals within 5 years or so, and your long-term goals in an appropriate amount of time (longer than 5 years). So, you may have to go through this process a few times until you are satisfied it works.

First, set up the first chart on page 37 ("Wrestling Your Monthly Expenses") so that it reflects your monthly expenses by category. (Use the work you did in the "How much do you spend" section to calculate expenses by category.) The chart lists suggested categories and suggested guidelines for percentage of your net income for each category. Feel free to modify the categories and guidelines to fit your own experience. For example, you may live in a city where housing costs are particularly high, so that category may have to have a higher spending guideline than we've noted. On the other hand, your transportation or education costs may be lower. Adjust the guidelines to fit your life, with two caveats: the guideline percentages must add to 100%, and you want to leave something leftover each month to apply toward meeting your goals (we've suggested 10% of net income). At the bottom of the page, note your monthly net income (after all taxes and deductions) from the "How much do you earn" section. Use this monthly net income number to determine what percentage each of your monthly expense categories is of your net income. (Divide expense category by net income to determine the percentage). Is your percentage within your suggested guidelines? If you are higher than the guidelines, that category may be a place for you to reduce spending.

Once you have entered your expenses by category, total them at the bottom of the chart, then compare your total monthly expenses with your total monthly net income. We hope your net income will be greater than your expenses. The remainder (monthly net income minus monthly expenses) will be the amount you will have leftover each month to apply toward your short-, intermediate- and long-term goals.

Are you in shock? If you are like many people, it will be clear that you won't be able to meet many or any of your financial goals with your current expense levels.

And so, now we come to the crux of what makes a PMP work, and that is that you **MUST REDUCE AND CONTROL YOUR MONTHLY SPENDING AND/OR INCREASE YOUR MONTHLY INCOME IN ORDER TO GENERATE ENOUGH EXTRA INCOME EACH MONTH TO ACHIEVE YOUR FINANCIAL GOALS.** Said another way, you need to control spending (and, we hope, also increase your income) today, so that you can meet your goals tomorrow. If you do this, we are quite sure you will feel empowered and in command. You will say to yourself things like, "One less mocha latte today, that much closer to my cottage at the beach". It's an attitude adjustment that works like magic. "One less mocha latte today and I'm closer to being rich" does not really resonate, right? It's not specific enough to something you are prepared to sacrifice for. But, when you "reallocate" your spending to save toward a tangible, enticing goal, it doesn't feel like sacrifice. It feels like liberation and achievement.

So, how to reduce spending (or increase income) enough to meet your goals? You start by looking at every single thing you spent in your weekly trackers and ask, "Is this truly important, or can I cut it out?" "Truly important" means something different to everyone. That mocha latte may be truly important to you. If so, find other places to cut. There are a million ways to cut spending. We offer some of them in Appendix 1. There are fewer ways to increase income, unless it's time for your promotion and raise, or unless you have enough time to add an additional job to your week. We offer a few income ideas in Appendix 1 as well. Good luck and good hunting. Use the second chart on page 38 ("Action Plan to Reduce Expenses/Increase Income") to note the specific areas you can reduce expenses and increase income. Note specific dollar goals for each one.

Once you have wrestled your spending (and income) into line, complete the third chart on page 39 - your Personal Money Plan - that incorporates your spending cuts (and, if applicable, income increases). Note that you do not have to use the expense categories we suggest in the chart on page 39 - use categories that make sense for you. Ideally, as we indicated above, your monthly income will now more than cover your expenses, and will also cover contributions toward your short-, intermediate- and long-term goals, enough toward those goals such that you achieve your short-term goals within a year or so, your intermediate- term goals within 5 years or so, and your long-term goals in an appropriate amount of time (longer than 5 years).

The last step may be self-evident, but we'll say it anyway. Once you implement your PMP successfully, then you need to use the "leftover" dollars each month to achieve those goals. If your short-term goal is to pay down your credit card debt, then use the leftover dollars to pay down the debt over-and-above your minimum payment the next month. If you have enough left over to both meet that goal and also meet a longer term goal, set up a separate savings account for the longer term goal, until you have enough saved in the account to meet that goal. The central purpose of your PMP is to meet your financial goals, so please, have at them each month until you do.

Wrestling Your Monthly Expenses

Expenses By Category	Guideline (approx % of net income)	Monthly $ Expense	Actual % Net Income	Within Guidelines?
Housing-rent/mortg/prop tax	23%			
Utilities-telephone/cell/heat/ electric/sewer/ water/cable/wifi	10%			
Transportation – Fixed (payment/insurance)	10%			
Transportation – Variable gas, repair, pkg, tolls, transit	5%			
Food, Household, Toiletries	15%			
Health, Life, Medical, and Dental (Insurance & care)	4%			
Dependent Care	?			
Education	5%			
Clothing and Accessories	5%			
Home Upgrades/Furniture	5%			
Entertainment/Vacations/Dining Out	5%			
Stationery, Gifts, Office	3%			
	90%			
Total Monthly Expenses (add from above)				
Monthly Net Income (from previous worksheet)				
Amount left to meet goals (Income less expenses)	10%			

Action Plan To Reduce Expenses/Increase Income

1)

2)

3)

4)

5)

Personal Money Plan

To reach your financial goals, stay within these spending amounts every month.

Expenses By Category	Monthly $ Amount
Housing (rent/mortgage/property taxes)	
Utilities – telephone/cell/heat/electric/sewer/water	
Transportation – Fixed (payment/insurance)	
Transportation – Variable (gas, oil, repair, parking, tolls, transit)	
Food, Household, Toiletries	
Health, Life, Medical, and Dental (insurance/care)	
Dependent care	
Education	
Clothing and Accessories	
Home Upgrades/Furniture	
Entertainment/Vacations	
Cable TV and Internet	
Dining Out	
Stationery, Gifts, Office	
A. Total Expenses (add from above)	
B. Total Monthly Net Income (from prior worksheet)	
Amount available to reach goals (B minus A)	

SECTION III

YOUR MONTHLY TRACKING PROGRAM

1. Using Your Financial Plan

It's not enough to develop a Personal Money Plan and then just let it gather dust somewhere in the depths of your computer. Your PMP needs to be an active document that you review at least monthly. In order to insure that you are making progress toward your financial goals, you need to measure your progress every month. In this section, we will offer you some tools to help measure your progress.

The first, and maybe most important, tool is the first chart on page 44, comparing your actual expenses to your Plan, by category. You should continue to track all of your expenses. At the end of the month organize your expenses by category and include the category totals in the first chart below. Compare your expenses by category to your Plan. How did you do? Well? Excellent !! Not so well? Then go back category-by-category (and item by item using your tracking information) and determine where you can do better next month. Make a commitment to do better. (Remember that beach cottage/first home/new car ...) See Appendix 2 for questions to ask yourself before you spend.

The second chart on page 45 monitors your outstanding credit card debt and interest/fees you are paying. This does NOT include the credit card bills that you pay in full each month (since you have already accounted for those in your expense tracking). It only includes the charges you carry over and pay interest and fees on. We have included this chart because we want to emphasize how critical it is that you pay off those credit cards as soon as possible, and as your first priority, before working on other financial goals. Credit card companies charge ultra-high rates of interest and these bills will drown you in debt if you are not careful. The monthly payments are low, and seem quite manageable, until you realize that, by making only the monthly payments, you may be paying off that debt for years, or decades, or your entire life. At some point, the credit card companies will not let you charge any more things to your card(s), at which point you will have mountains of debt to pay off, and no ability to charge more to your cards. So, please, please, please do whatever you need to do to pay your credit card balances off in full and then only charge on the card(s) what you can pay in full each month. We know someone who did not trust herself to control her credit card spending. For her, the solution was to cut up the cards and pay for everything by cash or check. If that sounds like you, you may want to do that as well. In any event, monitor your progress in paying off those balances by completing the second chart each month and comparing each month's chart to the months before, to make sure those balances, interest payments and fees are being reduced every month, until they are gone.

The third chart on page 45 is a financial summary for the month. List your total spendable income (after taxes and deductions) for the month, total month's expenses, the amount you set aside to meet your financial goals (we have indicated some goals for illustration purposes - you should list your own personal goals), and the amount you used to pay off your outstanding credit card balances. Again, note that the paying off of the credit card balances may end up being all that you can do in a given month. Do that first, as you also find ways to decrease your expenses and increase your income. Doing all of those things in tandem will enable you to pay off the credit card balances much faster. Once that's done, start working on your goals, while making sure to keep your spending under control.

As a final note, we think you will find that your financial life is much more manageable if you have a good filing system. Just a box with file folders will do, since we would much rather you channel any excess income to meeting your financial goals, rather than to a fancy file cabinet! We've included suggestions for organizing your home files and tax files in Appendix 3 and Appendix 4. While you're at it, if you review your bills, statements and payments as you file them, you may identify income and/or expense items you may have overlooked.

Financial Plan Reality Check

Expenses By Category	Monthly PMP $ Amount	Actual $ Spent this Month	Difference
Housing (rent/mortgage/property taxes)			
Utilities – telephone/cell/heat/electric/sewer/water			
Transportation – Fixed (payment/insurance)			
Transportation – Variable (gas, oil, repair, parking, tolls, transit)			
Food, Household, Toiletries			
Health, Life, Medical, and Dental (insurance/care)			
Dependent care			
Education			
Clothing and Accessories			
Home Upgrades/Furniture			
Entertainment/Vacations/Dining Out			
Cable TV and Internet			
Stationery, Gifts, Office			
A. Total Expenses (add from above)			
B. Total Monthly Net Income (from prior worksheet)			
Amount available to reach goals (B minus A)			

Outstanding Credit Card Debt Summary

End of Month_____ Current Credit Card Debt

Credit Card	Current Balance	Your more than minimum payment	Pay off time (use financial calculator)	Current interest rate
Credit Card 1				
Credit Card 2				
Credit Card 3				

End of Month Financial Summary

End of Month_____ Financial Summary

Monthly Amounts:	Planned $ Amount	Actual $ Amount	$ Difference
A. Spendable Income (after taxes/deductions)			
B. Total Expenses for Month			
C. Amount Available to Meet Goals (A minus B)			
Month Contributions to Goals			
Goal 1			
Goal 2			
Goal 3			
Month Contribution to Debt Payoff			
Credit Card 1			
Credit Card 2			
Loan 1			
Loan 2			

We wish you much success with your Personal Money Plan.
May all your goals be realized, while you lose your financial anxiety
and gain confidence, relief, control, and peace of mind.
Good luck !!
Enjoy !!

APPENDICES

Appendix 1 – How To Reduce Spending/Increase Income

Make your family/loved ones part of the process
If you are single and preparing your Personal Money Plan on your own, you will have sole control over your progress toward your financial goals. However, if you live with a spouse/significant other and/or have children, how you view your approach to your PMP will set the tone. Will you encourage your family to live well on a budget, or will they be stuck on regretting what they used to spend and resent and resist changes? Strategies to help them get with the program:

1. Be honest but upbeat. Tell them you are reducing spending to save for specific financial goals.
2. Ask them to help you find ways to save. Respond positively to their efforts and implement their suggested strategies where they make sense.
3. Ask them to step up. Maybe they can prepare/cook simple, delicious, low cost meals, or look through store coupons for you in mailings or online, for things you buy routinely.

Food Cost Reduction Strategies
1. Organize your dinners a week in advance to avoid eating out
2. Do inexpensive take-out nights: pizza night, Chinese night (order 1 or more fewer dishes than the number of eaters); deli-sandwich night (order from local grocery store or make yourself – 2 people can often share one huge sandwich) with chips or deli salad(s)
3. For dinners out, look for ethnic restaurants with good food at low prices. Avoid beverages out, other than water. Have a drink before going out, and one when you return.
4. Grocery strategies:
    a. Don't buy drinks in bottles – use a refrigerator filter or Brita water instead; SodaStream instead of buying soda or club soda
    b. Buy bread on sale – it can be frozen and toasted one slice at a time
    c. Trader Joe's for wine bargains
    d. Don't buy just because it's on sale, but do look for sale items that you will use anyway
    e. Target "Up and Up" store brand for many items: dryer fabric softener sheets, paper towels, toilet paper, sandwich bags, trash bags, facial tissues, cotton puffs, cotton swabs and so on
    f. Big Box stores (for example, Costco) for bulk purchases or party purchases

Clothing Cost Reduction Strategies
1. Take a hard look at your wardrobe. Organize clothes by outfits. Determine a reasonable number of outfits. Buy only to fill in existing stock.
2. Do not "go shopping for bargains". That is, don't buy because it's on sale. However, once you decide that you need something, try to find it on sale.
3. Try consignment stores. They offer great bargains on "gently used" clothing.

Gift Cost Reduction Strategies

1. Instead of a pricey wine, give a beautiful candle, a jar of specialty honey, a bottle of gourmet olive oil, or some artisan soap. Find a beautiful box at a consignment or discount store and fill it with tissue and gourmet chocolate bars.

2. Set a holiday budget in total, then by person within the total.

Hair/Mani-Pedi/Toiletries Cost Reduction Strategies

1. Do mani/pedi's at discount salons. Can you go an extra week between?

2. Shop around for colorists/cutters to find best value. Can you go an extra week or two between?

3. Buy as many toiletries as possible at Target/other discounters. See what can be easily substituted for pricier versions you now use – shampoo, conditioner, toner, sunscreen, body lotion, face cleanser, dental floss, are all possibilities to find lower cost alternatives that work well at Target or similar.

Cell Phone and Internet

Do family plan for cell phone. Call internet provider and make sure you are paying only for the services you want.

Income Boosting Strategies

Is it time for a raise/promotion at work? Do some homework before approaching your boss. Prepare a document outlining your accomplishments, skills that are key for the business/profession, and any other considerations that are relevant. Approach your boss in a positive and energetic way. Good luck !

Do you have a hobby or pastime that you can turn into income? Items you make can be sold online. If you have something you can teach in adult education programs, they are often offered during evenings and weekends. If you have a flair for interior design, or golf, or technology, or whatever, you might offer your services as a consultant. (Make sure you have not signed a contract with your primary employer that precludes you from working elsewhere).

Do you have extra space in your home? Consider a tenant, or AirBNB or the like, to generate rental income.

Don't forget that almost all income is taxable. You may be required to pay estimated taxes on any income that is not subject to withholding by an employer.

Share your Strategies

If you have good spending reduction or income boosting strategies, please let us know. We may include them in a future edition of this workbook. Email us at info@capitalwise.org.

Appendix 2 – Sticking To Your Budget
22 Questions To Ask Yourself Before You Spend

Do I really need it?	Can I get this for free?
Have I asked someone else for their opinion?	How long do I have to work to pay for this and is it worth it?
Am I buying it because it's on sale?	Will this help me reach my financial goals?
Can I negotiate the price?	Is this purchase going to increase or decrease in value?
Can I borrow it from someone instead of buying it?	Will I have to reduce my spending somewhere else to get this and stay in budget?
If I need to buy this, can I buy it with cash instead of my credit card?	Am I really going to eat/cook this before it expires?
Can I buy it for less money somewhere else?	Do I really need all of these (when buying in bulk)
Can I buy it for less money if I wait?	On a scale of 1 to 10 where 10 is ecstatic, how happy does this purchase make me?
Is it in my budget?	Can I buy something similar for less money?
Am I really going to wear this or use it?	Do I really need this now or can it wait?
Don't I have something like this?	Am I going to miss it if I don't have it?

Appendix 3 – Organizing Your Home Files

Checklist - What should you keep in your home files?

☐ Tax prep materials (see Appendix 4)

☐ Tax returns and related material for 6 years

☐ Bank statements for 3 years

☐ Statements of other investments, including 401(k) plans and IRA's for 3 years

☐ Student loan information and documentation; proof of payment

☐ Warranties and info about large purchases (appliances, televisions, computers, furniture, and so on) - for the life of the item

☐ Insurance policies and payment records

☐ Car related records - deeds, purchase/lease info, repair info - until car is sold or returned to lessor

☐ Receipts/credit card bills/checks paid for all home improvements - until tax return is filed after property is (eventually) sold

☐ Personal information and documents: Social Security card, passport, immunization records, copies of driver's license, copies of credit and debit cards - update as needed

☐ Contract copies

☐ Lease agreement, if renting, at least until rental period ends

☐ House closing materials, if home is owned, at least until house is sold and taxes paid for the year it sold

☐ Mortgage materials, if home is owned, at least until mortgage is paid

☐ Credit card bills paid - retain as desired, but keep tax-related bills (see Appendix 3)

☐ Utility bills paid - for 2 years, or as desired to monitor cost increases (or decreases)

☐ Other bills paid - for 2 years, or as desired

☐ Health records and medical bills - as desired

☐ Employee benefit information - until expired

Appendix 4 – Organizing Your Tax Files

**Please check irs.gov and your state tax division,
for additional guidelines that may pertain to your tax situation.**

Checklist - Current Year Tax Materials you will need for your tax returns

☐ W-2 forms from employers

☐ 1099 forms for non-employment (eg, consulting) income

☐ Tax statements from banks and brokerage firms

☐ Bank statements or credit card bills proving charitable donations

☐ Letters from charities confirming donations

☐ Letter from mortgage bank with mortgage/home equity interest paid

☐ Documentation of any student loan interest paid

☐ Canceled checks with any real estate taxes paid

☐ If self employed, or have rental income:

    ☐ Business-related expense receipts

    ☐ Business office expense documentation

☐ If applicable, K-1 forms for partnership income/loss

☐ If applicable, closing statements from real estate transactions

☐ If applicable, documentation of significant medical expenses

Retention - see irs.gov and your state tax division webpage for information and guidance regarding how long you should retain tax documents.

Appendix 5 – Weekly Expense Tracker

Week of _____

Date	Amount	Transaction		Date	Amount	Transaction
Mon.				**Thurs.**		
Tues.				**Friday**		
Wed.				**Sat./Sun**		

Appendix 6 - Monthly Expense Tracker

End of Month_____
Total Expenses from Weekly Tracking

Expenses By Category	Week 1	Week 2	Week 3	Week 4	Total
Housing (rent/mortgage/property taxes)					
Utilities – telephone/cell/heat/electric/sewer/water/cable tv/internet					
Transportation – Fixed (payment/insurance)					
Transportation – Variable (gas, oil, repair, parking, tolls, transit)					
Food, Household, Toiletries					
Health, Life, Medical, and Dental (insurance/care)					
Dependent Care					
Education					
Clothing and Accessories					
Home Upgrades/Furniture					
Entertainment/Vacations/Dining Out					
Stationery, Gifts, Office					
Other					
Other					
Other					
Total Expenses for Month of:_____					

About Us

CapitalWise Educational Services LLC was founded by a team of financial services professionals who are devoted to assisting individuals to navigate in today's financial world.

In doing our consulting and educational work, we looked for a clear, straightforward workbook to use to help our clients understand and manage their financial lives. All of the books we found were complicated and lengthy. So, we decided to write one ourselves.

We hope you will find this workbook to be helpful and clear. We welcome your feedback and look forward to hearing your stories. You can email us at info@capitalwise.org.

Our co-founders are:

Maria Antokas

Maria is a former banker and management consultant, and current educator, with over 30 years of business and consumer banking experience. She has a B.A. from Barnard College and an M.A. in Economics from New York University. A mother of two grown sons, Maria lives with her husband in the Maryland suburbs of Washington, DC.

Barbara Pagos

Barbara has 30+ years in managerial and executive positions on Wall Street and for a Fortune 50 company, and is a former trustee of two non-profits. She is a graduate of Smith College and has an MBA from Harvard Business School. Barbara has three grown children, and lives with her husband in the New Jersey suburbs of New York City.

CapitalWise Educational Services LLC does not provide legal, accounting, tax, investment, insurance or banking advice.